KEVIN DURANT

From Underdog to MVP

John Emerson

KEVIN DURANT

Table of Contents

INTRODUCTION

"I know that hard work got me here. And the day I stop working hard, this can all go away." – Kevin Durant

2014 NBA MVP AWARD ACCEPTANCE CEREMONY. It was the 2014 season, a time where up and coming superstars were rising to take reins of the league. New faces were all becoming the talk of the league, with no one player having fully cemented his control over the NBA landscape. The Steph Currys, James Hardens, and the Kawhi Leonards of the world were popping up all over the league, making names for themselves as soon-to-be formidable players who were going to carry the league in the years to come. However, amongst all those players that year, one had shone the brightest and had officially solidified his place in NBA history – immortalizing his young but already storied legacy.

His name was Kevin Durant.

Kevin was in a special position. He had been drafted before all those other young players whom were rising through the ranks, but also after all the other, already-established NBA legends such as LeBron James and Kobe Bryant. This marked him as alone in his quest for NBA greatness. Drafted back in the 2007 NBA Draft as a lanky, tall kid out of the University Of Texas, he had a unique skill set unlike any other player the world had ever seen.

A 7 foot Small Forward who could dribble the ball with amazing skill, sprint up and down the court with graceful versatility, and shoot 35-foot jumpers similar to a shooting guard, Durant was primed for success at an early age. After just seven short years in the NBA, he would prove them right. However, Kevin's future wasn't always so certain. Those seven years were filled with trials, tribulations and doubts that he had to endure and outlast – but he finally emerged triumphant.

Crowds of basketball fans, especially fans of the Oklahoma City Thunder, had tuned in to the live broadcast to see this young basketball star finally cement his place in the NBA's history books. Finally, the announcer broke the suspense: "The 2013-14 Kia NBA Most Valuable Player Award, Kevin Durant!"

Kevin walked up slowly towards the podium, relishing every single step he took – enjoying the momentous occasion he had worked so hard to achieve. His teammates on stage with him rose up in a standing ovation, while the crowds of fans below the stage followed suit. Across the world, fans whom were watching live joined in the applause for the young basketball talent that they had grown to love and respect..

Kevin had built up his reputation as a very likeable and favorable player amongst the fans in the league. In only seven years, he had established an unprecedented ability to score better than any other player, winning multiple scoring titles. His highlight reels drew in fans from all over the basketball world, as fans loved witnessing Durant hit clutch game winners for his team and throw down amazing dunks on opponents in astounding fashion. Within just five years in the league, he even led the Thunder to the NBA Finals - an accomplishment applauded throughout the league by analysts and fans alike, as the Thunder had still been just a newly established team at the time. For any player, let alone a relatively young one like Kevin, to be able to pull off such a feat was definitely remarkable. Although the Thunder eventually lost to LeBron James and his Miami Heat, many people knew that it was only the beginning for Kevin, and that he would have a long career ahead of him with many more chances to claim the basketball's ultimate prize.

Although he had failed to claim the NBA Championship years before, he put his setbacks aside for that very day, as it marked a special occasion for Kevin: he had successfully clinched the highest honor in basketball for any individual player. The millions of die-hard fans he had amassed throughout his career had tuned in to watch their favorite superstar claim the NBA's Most Valuable Player Award.

"Wow" was the first word out of Durant's mouth as he took the podium – almost in shock himself at how far he had come in his time as a basketball player. Even in receiving the highest of honors, he found himself being humble and almost shy of the limelight, but on such a special occasion, he knew he had to embrace the moment.

Kevin would go on to give one of the most famous MVP speeches in league history, showcasing his humble and gracious spirit. He would thank each of his teammates individually, telling them how much they meant to him and that he could not have achieved what he had without their support. As he went through his list of teammates, friends and family, everyone could sense the rise of emotion throughout the room. Kevin began to shed a tear while at the podium. The world was witnessing a superstar at the peak of his game with all the glories of the world given to him, vulnerable and exposed. For the first time, they were seeing a side of Kevin that no one had seen before, and were witnessing an aspect of his life outside of the basketball court that was just as precious as basketball itself. As he checked each person's name off his thank you list, he grew increasingly vulnerable as the emotions flowed through him, unable to be contained.

Fans in attendance were cheering him on as he tried his best to maintain his composure – possibly having found a new admiration and respect for their superstar. Everyone understood just why Kevin was feeling so much emotion in that moment, as he had gone through a rough and difficult upbringing as a child. Being brought up by a single parent, almost always on the brink of poverty, circumstances looked bleak for Kevin as the prospects of earning a better life for him and his family were all but a pipe dream. Yet despite immense adversity growing up, he somehow managed to find himself on basketball's biggest stage, being bestowed basketball's highest honor. Only once he began his speech did it finally dawn on him: he had finally made it. All those years of hardship had led him to have a rough and tough exterior, but after 25 long and cruel years of battling, he had finally led his guard down - all the decades of pent up emotions finally broke free.

CHAPTER ONE

THE REAL MVP

"My mom just wants to make sure that my heart is always in whatever I do and I'm in things for the right reasons." – Kevin Durant

KEVIN AND HIS FAMILY HAD BEEN THROUGH so much throughout his formative years. Moving from house to house, living off food stamps, and forever being on shaky ground, Kevin never knew what the future held. Yet throughout all those times, his single mother had always been the glue that held Kevin and his siblings together – being firm when she needed to, but tender during softer and more subtler moments of their life.

By a certain point in his speech, Kevin had already lost all hope for regaining any sense of composure as he checked off the last few remaining people on his thank you list. There was one person left on the list – his mother. Kevin looked straight into her eyes as they brimmed with pride – the same eyes that had witnessed her baby boy's rise to superstardom.

"I don't think you know what you did," Kevin told her, choking on his words in the process. "The odds were stacked against us – a single parent with 2 boys by the time you were 21 years old. " His mother had already covered her face, trying to hide her own emotions.

"Everybody told us we weren't supposed to be here," Kevin continued with all the strength he could muster. "You made us believe, you kept us off the streets, put clothes on our backs, food on the table." Everyone could sense the build up of emotions once more, just when they thought that there were no more tears left to be shed. "When you didn't eat, you made sure we ate. You went to sleep hungry. You sacrificed for us."

All the weight of those 25 years of hardship had converged into that one single moment for Kevin and his mother, revealing all of their pains and battle scars to the rest of the world. In one final cathartic release of emotion, Kevin muttered the words that caused all the pain and struggle to finally drain out from underneath them, bringing audiences all over the world to their feet as they shared in their celebration:

"You're the real MVP."

CHAPTER TWO

EARLY CHILDHOOD

"Hard work beats talent when talent fails to work hard." – Kevin Durant

KEVIN DURANT'S CHILDHOOD WAS ANYTHING BUT ORDINARY GROWING UP. Having had to go through immense battles of poverty, starvation and lack of resources just to keep his head above water, he was exposed to hardships and trials at an extremely young and tender age. Kevin had been born to a dysfunctional family; his father Wayne Pratt walked out he was still an infant. Alone, young and helpless, Kevin's mother Wanda was faced with the unthinkable task of raising her children all by herself with no husband, job or support system around her. Desperate for help, she turned to Kevin's grandmother Barbara Davis for help – who fortunately accepted.

Like many other young families being brought up and raised in the slums of America, the prospect of leaving poverty and starting a better life were slim and in some cases even impossible. A good education was hard to come by for such children, and even if they were enrolled in good schools, the environment in which they were brought up in made it even more difficult for them to excel in their studies and build a better future for themselves. Wanda knew all this; she was hell-bent on making sure her children did not succumb to that very fate. Determined to defeat the stereotype that single mothers could not raise successful children, she would personally make sure she provided the best for her children, as she knew that they were her only hope for a brighter future out of poverty. It was during those times where the Durant family faced the darkness of constant hardships, but left with no other choice, all they had to do was keep moving forward – with Wanda leading the charge.

Kevin's ability for basketball was already evident at a young age. With him being naturally tall but having the raw potential of a versatile guard, it was immediately obvious to Wanda that her son had an opportunity to become an exceptional player. Wanda would pull out all stops in making sure these prominent abilities her son possessed would not go to waste, as she spurred him on and trained him hard to develop his skills.

Because of this, Kevin would be exposed to the rigors of hard work unlike any other young basketball talent would face in his childhood. Being forced to wake up in the middle of the night during the summer time, he would be forced by his mother to ensure he stayed in peak physical condition by making him train and do various exercises such as pushups and even hill sprints. While the rest of the world was sleeping, Kevin was hard at work honing his craft – and it would be these early experiences that would shape Durant into having the discipline and work ethic which ultimately led him to being a superstar in the league today.

Kevin's games were always scrutinized by Wanda. She wanted to make sure that every last bit of potential was squeezed out of her son, and that his game would have no holes or weaknesses for his opponents to capitalize on. Screaming at the sidelines of his games, her training was brutal (yet necessary), integral for this young superstar in the making. As a kid, Kevin couldn't understand why he was being put through such immense torture at a young age. At times, the young Kevin even began to resent his mother for the torture she was putting him through. Little did he know that these early stages of learning the values of hard work and determination would pay massive dividends in the future, helping him earn his place on basketball's biggest stage.

Basketball was all Wanda had to ensure a brighter future for her children, and with all those years of sweat and hard work, Kevin's natural prowess began to blossom and develop – making him one of the brightest young basketball stars the nation had witnessed. This young star would also begin to shine some light on the once dark times the Durant family was constantly facing, as Kevin's father re-entered his life by the time he was a high school basketball player – even following him cross-country to basketball tournaments. With Kevin's young basketball career finally starting to gain traction, and with old family wounds finally starting to heal, things were finally starting to look better for the Durant family. However, just when it seemed as if they had finally caught a break, tragedy struck once again.

CHAPTER THREE

35

"I just want to grow spiritually with the Lord. I'm keeping strong at it, just trying to make my walk with faith a little better." – Kevin Durant

IN THE SPORTING WORLD OF MARKETING, media and fame, athletes go a long way to ensure their popularity sustains the test of time alongside their playing career. Endorsement deals and lucrative moneymaking business opportunities depend on the athlete leveraging their fame and star power to generate the most sales for themselves and for their brand. In a world where NBA players change their jersey numbers constantly for that very reason, Kevin Durant wears number 35 for a completely different one – as a reminder of the tragedy that struck him years ago, before he even entered the NBA.

Growing up without a father figure proved to be tough for Kevin. With his mother working tirelessly day and night to support her children, Kevin would sometimes find himself alone with no mentor in his life to guide him through the tough times. It was during those times that Charles Craig, Kevin's first basketball coach, entered into his life.

Kevin was only 8 years old when he first met Charles. Right from the instant they met, they formed a connection unlike any Kevin had experienced up until that point. The jovial and heartwarming personality of Charles immediately drew Kevin in and filled the hole in his life from his lack of a father figure - something that Kevin had longed for all his life. Charles was the first person to teach and instill the values of basketball in Kevin; he also taught him the values of life off the court. There were times where Kevin would spend entire days and nights with Charles, further building and forging a father-son like connection that Kevin had grown to love and treasure dearly. At a time when all was lost for Kevin, Charles stepped in with a love for the young superstar that would go on to shape him to be the man that he is today.

Despite his rise to fame and stardom as a young basketball phenom, Kevin never lost his grounding in his support system surrounding him. From a young age Kevin practiced humility in the face of success, which was further encapsulated by his loyalty to those close to him – in particular to Charles. Kevin accredited many of his successes to him and loved him with all his heart, but Kevin would soon learn the harsh rules of life at an early age - that not all relationships have a good ending: while Kevin was in the midst of his rising fame as a junior at Oak Hill Academy, Charles Craig was brutally shot and murdered.

Just when all seemed to be going well for Kevin, a part of his life was mercilessly taken away from him. His father figure was now gone forever, and all that was left of him were the memories of a young boy who had only managed to understand the meaning of friendship and love through that relationship. Needless to say, Kevin was devastated. His basketball coach and best friend had "died for nothing," Durant himself said. Till this day, Kevin carries the painful memories of Charles' death and life with him every single day. It may be a painful burden to bear, having to remember and recollect the tragedy that struck Kevin at such a tender age, but the young superstar in the making vowed to assume that burden for the rest of his life, however painful it might be.

Charles Craig died at the age of 35. This is what prompted Kevin to choose that for his jersey number; in this way Charles is with Kevin every single game that he steps onto a basketball court, as a reminder of the success he could not have achieved without him. Despite the pain of his loss, Kevin can only smile as he watches millions of fans around the world join him in wearing the same number, spreading the legacy of the one man that Durant would be forever indebted to.

https://www.flickr.com/photos/xtrah/6301043613/

CHAPTER FOUR

RISE TO STARDOM

"I don't know what I'm going to do tomorrow. I just know for sure I'm going to keep playing basketball." –
Kevin Durant

SEPTEMBER 14, 2013. Kevin's vehicle rolled up along the University Of Texas campus to the uproarious cheers of college students. It was hard to hear individual cheers amongst all the culmination of noise and chaos that surrounded Kevin's return back to his college campus. However, one chant could be heard amongst that entire ruckus: "K.D.! Thanks for coming back!"

Kevin could only smile, wave and high-five the occasional fan that walked up to him as he drove past them. He was like a rock star to his own alma mater, and now the students of University Of Texas were welcoming him back with open arms. Kevin had decided to drop by his old college for a special visit, and was humbled at the fanfare he had received. The hero's welcome was unsurprising: he single-handedly put the University Of Texas basketball team on the map while he was playing there. Though he only played for one year, that was all he had needed to make a name for himself and garner the mass attention of fans and scouts all over the world. Kevin had made many good memories in college, and he enjoyed walking down the hallways, reminiscing about his stepping-stones to stardom.

https://www.flickr.com/photos/9578077@N07/6067951519/

High School

Kevin Durant's official rise to stardom began in high school. Due to his shaky upbringing, Kevin was always moving from one home and apartment to another. The constant change of scenery was no stranger to him, and high school would be no different. He would start his high school basketball career with the National Christian Academy before moving to Oak Hill Academy. The constant movement in Kevin's life undoubtedly took its toll on him, but it did nothing to his game. All those years of blood, sweat and tears seemed to be paying off as he put on a show for his population of ever-growing fans. Those first three years of Kevin's career were not momentous or monumental, but they did lay the groundwork and the strong foundation for what would be a breakout year for his career.

Kevin's senior year in high school started

off shaky as well. He was forced to move once again, this time transferring to Montrose Christian High School; however, his basketball career would be anything but uncertain. He had grown nearly half a foot and was now standing at 6 feet, 7 inches, towering over all the other high school players. Usually, players who possess such an unfair height advantage typically would be balanced out with their lack of speed and often one-dimensional play. A player who stood out and above all the other players that much would be positioned at the front court, either as a back-to-the-basket type center or a power forward. But for Kevin, that would not be the case.

Not only did he possess the height advantage of a big man but the quickness and the ball handling skills of a guard, his reach and lengthy physique were also the overpowering tools he could utilize against his opponents, enabling him to shoot easily over them. Kevin was blessed with the perfect basketball physique, and he took every single advantage of it. Before the season even began, he had already committed to the University Of Texas, a testament to how much attention he was already getting from college scouts due to his level of play.

With his newly acquired basketball tools, as well as a college placing firmly intact, Kevin would go on to absolutely dominate the high school basketball scene, opening up a huge new wave of fans and media hype for the young talent to take in. Nobody had ever witnessed a player like Durant, with his wide array of skills and his physical dominance; he put on a show for his fans every single game he played, gathering accolades and achievements in the process.

At the end of his senior year, he was named the Washington Post All Met Basketball Player of The Year, and even clinched the Most Valuable Player Award at the 2006 McDonald's All American Game. K.D.'s hard work was finally beginning to pay off, and his name began to echo across high schools and colleges all across the nation. Slowly but surely, Kevin Durant was rising to stardom; for once, he could envision a brighter future for him and his family.

However, K.D. knew he could not let his newfound stardom go to his head. It was only the first step towards his ultimate goal of making it to the professional level, and he carried the humility he had always possessed in his personality even at the peak of his high school career. All the media attention had him now widely regarded as the second-best high school basketball prospect in the nation; that was the perfect platform for him to take the college basketball world by storm.

Naturally, wherever he went Kevin would face doubters. Being the oversized kid in high school, he could easily dominate his opponents and put on a show, but now many basketball analysts would wonder if K.D. would be able to have the same type of impact in college, where the bigger and much better players roamed. Kevin chose to not be deterred by the naysayers or doubters, and with his support system around him in the form of his family and friends, he remained focused on letting his game do most of the talking – or in this case, quieting the noise coming from the haters. College would only be a pit stop for this young superstar, but nobody figured that in just one short year, Kevin Durant would go from just a "talented high school kid" to "basketball's next biggest star."

CHAPTER FIVE

COLLEGE

"I just loved being in the gym. It was tough at times. Sometimes I wanted to quit, but I'm glad I stuck with it." – Kevin Durant

KEVIN HAD ALWAYS GROWN UP SHELTERED and protected in his small-knit community of family and friends. Despite constantly moving from one home to another during his upbringing, nothing had prepared him to move away from the people whom had always been beside him throughout his life up until that point. But like a hero ready to take on the road of adventure, Kevin knew it was finally his time to say goodbye.

He would be a long way away from home. The fanfare and success he had built up in high school was now ready to slingshot him into the trenches of college basketball – a whole new world, with brand new experiences that the young talent could not wait to conquer. He was now one step closer towards the NBA dream and to bringing prosperity and wealth to his family. All he had to do was go through one more trial – one that would determine just whether he was truly ready to summit basketball's highest mountain. If the NBA was the peak, then college would be the base camp – and it would be here that he would gather the necessary resources to start his expedition to the top. The University of Texas awaited him.

16th January 2007. The University of Texas basketball team was matched up against Oklahoma State University, an old but adversarial rival. It was Kevin Durant's first year in college, and as a freshman he had already surpassed and exceeded the expectations of even the harshest of sports critics. Usually, freshman players start off their playing years slowly earning their minutes coming off the bench, learning as much as they could before fully taking on a full-time role for their team. Yet Kevin was anything but a "usual" player. Ever since he had been born, his life had been extraordinary; as he matured, he had developed a physique and skill set that were extraordinary. Everyone on his team knew that from the moment Kevin stepped onto the court, he would grow into a leadership role; true enough, in his freshman year, he was thrust into that very position almost immediately.

Most players would crumble under such high expectations and pressure at such an early age, but all those years of hard work with his mother and family had primed him for just about any situation. He was now fully equipped and prepared to take on that very challenge. Even being miles away from his family, the habits, discipline and basketball prowess that he picked up from his early years were clearly resonating with his playing style and were evident in his highlights. Against Oklahoma State University, it would be no different.

"Woah! The dunk by Durant! And you're gonna be hearing that name a ton tonight – Kevin Durant." The commentator foreshadowed the series of events that were going to play out for that game, and he did so with an uncanny accuracy. Kevin's first basket against his opponent was an emphatic breakaway dunk, almost sending a message to the booing Oklahoma State crowd that he had arrived - and he had arrived to win.

Sending a message to the OSU fans would

be an understatement. Kevin would put on a show that would leave fans, critics and analysts at the edge of their seats throughout the entire game and would leave them buzzing for the rest of the season.

Fast forward to the 4th quarter. The slow, steady chants of the Oklahoma State University fans spurring on their team were filling the stadium, as they could sense the finish line in plain sight. There were about 90 seconds left in the game, and the University Of Texas had found themselves down by 5 points, to a delighted enemy crowd trying so desperately to boo them out of their stadium. However, what was supposed to be an easy win for the OSU team would be anything but. What would unfold for the next few minutes would be a testament to the greatness of Kevin Durant's college career – and the OSU fans were the unfortunate victims of his apparent onslaught.

The Texas Longhorns were desperate for a

chance to stay in the game, and they turned to their young leader to guide them along the way. He had already amassed a number of points through a series of tough jump shots, dunks and lay ups – all with the OSU guards throwing whatever defense they had at him to no avail. Even the commentators for the OSU home fans were showering praise on Durant: "This young man is a supernova. He is a multi-faceted scorer who gets to the rack, bury a three, embarrass you on the block, and best of all – he is unselfish, sometimes more so than need be."

However, K.D. had no choice but to be selfish. His team had turned to him for his heroics to save the day, and he would have to deliver.

CHAPTER SIX

FULL-FLEDGED STAR

"I always want to win because I never want to sit out on the sidelines outside." – Kevin Durant

"DURANT, DRIVING LEFT, FLIPS IT UP... GOT IT!" The announcer shrieked in excitement as Durant had started to single-handedly take over the game – cutting the OSU lead by two.

The OSU fans began to sweat, this time not from excitement but from the anxiety that the Longhorns might come back to steal the game away from them. For a moment, the crowd tasted relief as one of their players came back with a ferocious dunk to answer K.D.'s personal heroics. But just like how they had an answer for Durant's offensive attacks, K.D. would make sure he had an answer of his own.

"Durant.. A long, long three... YES!" Kevin Durant scored a long 3-pointer, stunning the OSU fans and players once more. The game was tied, and what was supposed to be a victory for OSU with seconds left on the clock was about to turn into an all-out battle for the ages.

The game went into overtime. The crowd was louder than ever, with emotions spilling over from the mix of excitement and anxiety. The game was extremely close, and K.D. was still not done with his onslaught.

The Longhorns caught themselves being down by two once again with only seconds left to spare in the game. However, the announcer broke the spirits of fans across the nation as he exclaimed, "Here's Durant with the catch and shoot... HE BURIES IT!"

K.D. rolled around the screen and calmly knocked down a fade away jump shot to tie the game. He was truly unguardable, and he was fully in the zone as he nailed another cold-blooded clutch shot right in his opponent's face, much to the dismay of the home crowd OSU fans. Tensions were at their peak, but the game was still far from over; the two teams simply could not shake each other off. With K.D.'s personal heroics and OSU's own weaponry, the game entered into a second overtime.

By then fans from across the nation had already tuned in after hearing of K.D.'s brilliance being displayed in such an exciting game. At that point, the entire arena knew Durant was nowhere near done with his in-game brilliance as he continuously scored clutch shot after clutch shot for his team, with each shot stinging more than the previous ones. The Longhorns so desperately depended on him to stay alive, and in the second overtime, they once again found themselves down three with only about a minute left in the game.

Once again, Kevin would deliver. "Durant.... Long distance.... A THREE POINTER! AND LOOK AT THIS WE ARE TIED AGAIN!" The once chaotic ruckus from the fans had dropped to absolute silence, which the announcer broke with excitement at what he was witnessing. The OSU fans simply could not put what their thoughts into words, and mixed with their emotions of dismay and heartbreak, they were left silent.

What they were actually witnessing was a once in a lifetime spectacle – the birth of greatness for a young player. Without an accurate way to describe that greatness, there was simply nothing else to do but stare in admiration as K.D. hit yet another cold-blooded shot to tie the game.

"Not again," the fans thought, as it seemed like whatever OSU was throwing at the Longhorns was simply not working. Durant had an answer for every challenge, no matter how tough it seemed to be. There was now a mix of hatred and admiration towards Kevin Durant as the young freshman assumed the burden of his entire team and came through in the clutch, time and time again, with no hesitation or any sense of cowardice. Kevin's face took on a scowl-like countenance; just like a superstar, he had grown to be absolutely fearless in the face of adversity.

The game had now gone to its third overtime. The Longhorns, OSU and the stadium were mentally and physically exhausted from all the tension the last few hours had entailed for them. Third overtime games are rare in any level of basketball, let alone college basketball, but K.D. was far from relinquishing control and victory over the game. Whenever it seemed like OSU was going to easily walk away with a victory, Durant mercilessly broke their hearts with a series of difficult daggers that had only escalated and enlarged the bubble of tension that was begging to be burst so badly.

The OSU fans were now clinging for yet another chance to win, being up by two with about 15 seconds left to the game. But as history had shown throughout the course of that day, the game would be far from over. The Longhorns had been trailing throughout most of the game even with Durant's late game heroics keeping them alive; the Longhorns were trying with an ever-growing persistence to finally take control of the game and lead OSU. After three overtimes of effort, K.D. and his team would finally break through.

There were only seconds left in the game.

The OSU crowd held whatever was left of their breath as Kevin's teammate drove towards the center of the lane and put up a floater to try and potentially tie the game. The suspense and tension in the room reached its peak as the ball hovered at its apogee, only to hit the back of the rim. For a split second, the OSU fans breathed a collective sigh of relief – but they had forgotten about Durant, who had hustled to get in position underneath the basket, grabbing the rebound with whatever reserves of energy he had left.

"Durant...FOULED ON THE PLAY! HE MADE THE BASKET - HE'll GO TO THE LINE!"

Breakthrough.

It was as if the fans and announcers could have just collapsed from the heat and the weight of that very moment. A clutch shot was a rare spectacle to behold for most games, but Kevin Durant had just made four of them in one massive highlight reel for the ages. The Longhorns had been struggling to stay close to OSU, but now K.D. had finally gotten them over the hump, leading them to take the lead.

CHAPTER SEVEN

UNDERDOG

"I'm not a guy that's going to brag or feel like I'm better than the group." – Kevin Durant

THAT GAME AGAINST OSU WAS TRULY indicative of Kevin Durant's character and spirit. He had always been the underdog, always fought and struggled to stay alive by any means necessary despite huge adversity for his entire life. Yet no matter how tough the circumstances may seem, Kevin was never going to give up and cave in.

No matter what doors were closed or shut

off to him in his life, he would never relent, hammering on that shuttered door day-in and day-out until it finally came crashing down. Even though if it took three gruelling and tiring overtimes to do so, he was not going to let circumstances dictate the outcome of his life - he certainly didn't let it dictate the outcome of that game. What was supposed to be a sure victory for OSU had gone the ultimate distance – showing just how far Durant was willing to go to become victorious both on and off the court.

If there was any doubt as to whether Kevin belonged in the college ranks, he certainly shattered all of them at that very moment as he showcased his full arsenal at crucial times when his team needed him most.

K.D. walked up to the free throw line to complete the 3-point play. He had battled non-stop to get his team to take the lead, and now he was finally going to be able to do so.

He knocked down the free throw, surprising nobody, and calmly backpedaled his way into defense.

"Man, is he cool," the announcer nonchalantly mustered up those words to describe the greatness that he had just witnessed. "Cool" would be an ironic understatement: he had been on fire and unstoppable throughout the entire course of the game. "Cool" simply would not suffice anymore as an accurate description of Kevin Durant.

K.D. wasn't just cool; he was a superstar.

https://www.flickr.com/photos/xtrah/6301042891/

CHAPTER EIGHT

THE SUMMIT

"I look at my jersey and see the NBA logo, I'm like, 'I didn't think I'd be here'." – Kevin Durant

KEVIN ENTERED THE ROOM TO A SWARM OF REPORTERS all waiting eagerly to greet him. He had been used to the fanfare and attention he got from his games, but never was he exposed to so much media attention in such a short span of time. He took a deep breath and proceeded to sit down as the reporters began bombarding the young college prospect with questions on him entering the NBA.

It was 2007, and Kevin was probably the youngest player to have declared for the 2007 NBA Draft after only one year in college. Most college prospects would spend at least 2 to 3 years in college, developing their game further to a point where they felt ready to join the elite ranks of the NBA. Kevin was the exception. He had always felt ready – as if his dream of entering the NBA was inevitable. In just one year, he had made history as a freshman for the Texas Longhorns. The 18-year-old kid out of Washington, DC had risen to unbelievable superstardom, and with all the highlights, accolades and achievements backing him up, he was nothing if not confident about his decision to leave college after a year and pursue his biggest goal head on. He had dreamt of that moment ever since he was a kid. All of those years, all the training, sweating, praying, crying, all simply for a chance at a better life for his family, finally seemed to come true.

"Whether I'm one, two, three or four or five or whatever. Whatever happens, it's going to be a dream, and I'm gonna ask somebody to pinch me – hopefully I don't wake up," Kevin replied to one of the reporter's questions sheepishly, to the smiles of everyone else in the room.

When asked about which draft position he thought he would get picked for, Kevin simply wasn't concerned about the outcome. He was an 18-year-old kid who loved basketball as much as he loved his family; with insurmountable amounts of hard work over the years, he was finally able to combine both of his loves – taking both his game and his family's life situation to the next level.

It was a magical moment for Kevin – perfectly encapsulated when David Stern announced his name: "With the 2nd pick in the 2007 NBA Draft, the Seattle Supersonics select Kevin Durant from the University of Texas."

Sonics fans from all over the country cheered. They knew they had just gotten a fresh start for their struggling franchise. With all the media hype that surrounded Kevin in college, he was the perfect starting piece for a Seattle franchise that was begging for a new superstar to give them hope. His time in college, although short, had been nothing short of spectacular – being the only freshman to win the Naismith College Player Of The Year Award. And just like his first year in college, he would once again have to fill the shoes and responsibilities of being a young, talented leader for a team looking so desparately for guidance – shoes that would fit him perfectly, and mold him into an ever bigger superstar than he already was.

Rookie Year

As a rookie and the franchise player for a rebuilding team, K.D. would excel on all fronts, finishing the year with averages of

20.3 points, 4.4 rebounds, 2.4 assists and 1 steal per game – joining LeBron James and Carmelo Anthony as the only teenagers in NBA history to average at least 20 points per game in a season. Right from his early years, he was already in good company – joining the other elite rookies that had come before him and were now dominating the league. Everybody knew it would only be a matter of time before Durant broke out of his shell and exploded into the NBA scene with full gusto and determination. Yet for his first few years, he went relatively unnoticed. The kid from college was quietly building up his repertoire as the main man in Seattle, all waiting to burst onto the NBA scene with a bang – announcing his arrival as a superstar. He had already made heads turn as a rookie in Seattle with his familiar array of highlights – one of which was a beautiful fade away three-pointer game winner against the Atlanta Hawks in double overtime – reminiscent of his amazing clutch performance in college against OSU.

But for the most part, the league was busy paying attention to the other more successful teams who were dominating at the time. That didn't matter for Durant, as his first year was spent purely on honing his skills and building up his own role as the leader – having a perfect ending with Kevin winning the Rookie Of The Year Award.

Oklahoma City Thunder

Similar to his demeanor, K.D.'s first year was relatively quiet. Nobody doubted the potential the young baller had, but he had still not made a definitive mark in the league apart from being named Rookie of The Year. Although quiet, he had always let his game do most of the talking for him – and when the Seattle franchise decided to pack up and relocate to Oklahoma as a brand new team, this fresh start was the perfect timing for Kevin to explode onto the basketball scene, letting his game cause shockwaves of excitement throughout the league.

With a new exciting skill set to display and a new uniform to compliment it, Kevin Durant dominated the NBA landscape with a brilliant second-year performance. Kevin was getting better as each year went by. The scariest part of it all was the fact that he was still only a relatively young teenager with so much more potential and room left to grow – and yet he had already established himself as a formidable scorer in any situation on the court.

His amazing and extravagant highlights were often balanced with his humility off the court, and he soon quickly gained a reputation of being the "nice guy" in the NBA. Yet this nice guy persona was not to be underestimated; he was just as ferocious as any other player he matched up against on the court – ruthless in his scoring to will his team to victories.

https://www.flickr.com/photos/keithallison/12262708196/

In the next couple of seasons, Kevin had already gathered a whole new plethora of accolades to his name. He had set the Rookie Challenge scoring record at a remarkable 46 points and showcased his familiar late game heroics to once again bring his team over the hump and win the game. In just his third year, he was also selected for his first All-Star game, and had led his newly formed team to their first playoff berth – shocking the doubters in the process. Not only was K.D. selected to the All-NBA team, but he also became the youngest scoring champion in

NBA history – a true testament to the effortlessness that Kevin seemed to pull off his amazing achievements with. The young superstar was clearly making the NBA his home, and for these first few years he really let himself get comfortable building his fandom and taking his reputation and game to new heights. The young kid from Washington had achieved his biggest dream of making it to the NBA, and of bringing prosperity and wealth to his family.

However, after those few years of initial enjoyment wore off, Durant was finally ready to pack his bags once more and summit another bigger, better, yet tougher mountain - the one insurmountable challenge that has either made or broken NBA players' legacies throughout the history of the league. The one achievement that every other NBA player in the league has had their eyes, hearts and hopes set upon, and yet the one thing where only one team would be blessed enough to hold and claim it as their own each year: the NBA championship.

CHAPTER NINE

A NEW GOAL

"I'm just trying to grow. That's one thing I told myself is, 'Don't worry about who people say is the best player."
– Kevin Durant

THE OKLAHOMA CITY THUNDER HAD ALREADY MADE their first playoff berth with K.D. and other key players on their team, such as Russell Westbrook and Jeff Green, However, their playoff runs were far from successful. Their first had them up against one of the top teams in the West with one of the best players in the world. Suddenly, the fun and games that came from his first couple of years of cruising through the league had all but dissipated, as Kevin experienced a rude awakening to the real realm of NBA greats.

2010 NBA Playoffs, Western Conference Quarter Finals Game 1. The young and excited Thunder squad, led by their young and excited franchise player, had just shocked the world by qualifying for the playoffs despite being less than five years old in the league. K.D.'s brand and reputation had already been established as a remarkable scoring phenom and was growing rapidly each day. With key additions to his team, Kevin finally had enough of a supporting cast to contend for an NBA title – a privilege only given to a select few. However, unlike all the other times Kevin had breezed through challenges with his natural playing prowess, the young star and his even younger team would be halted in their tracks to be sent crashing down to earth after their meteoric and seemingly effortless rise to prominence.

Their first big test had arrived – and it spared no expense in dismantling the young Durant's naïve title dreams. They were up against the defending champions, the Los Angeles Lakers, which were led by perennial superstar and all-around basketball legend Kobe Bryant. This series would introduce to K.D. and his team a completely new level of play that was unknown to them - one that only the elite teams had learnt to acquire, and only familiar to a blessed number of teams throughout NBA history. This level of play was the one required to climb and conquer the NBA's greatest prize: the Larry O'Brien Trophy. It would be a rude awakening to the Thunder; their easy ride turned out to be quite the opposite once they faced off against the top dogs on basketball's biggest and most intense stage.

The Oklahoma City Thunder had found themselves trailing throughout the entire game. It seemed like whatever big game

Kevin was a part of, he would always have to bring his team back from a deficit rather than lead his opponent in the first place. Whether be it in college games or NBA games, that seemed to be a familiar trend for Kevin – indicative of how he had always been an underdog his entire life, forced to battle back against all odds to succeed. Now, in the NBA playoffs, it would be no different. Just like all the other times he and his team were down, the Thunder would call on number 35 to will them back to victory – only this time, Kevin would be far from victorious.

Early stages of the 3rd quarter and the Lakers were leading with a comfortable 8-point lead, being relatively in control from the opening tip-off. Kobe and his team had put on a series of highlights consisting of dunks, fade-aways and other tough shots, all to the dismay of the Thunder. The barrage of attacks by the Lakers had stunned Oklahoma momentarily, and Durant was desparately trying to put on his cape and play hero ball as he had always done throughout his career.

K.D. had intercepted a pass thrown by Derek Fisher of the Lakers and was sprinting down the court with all his might to finish the play. The Thunder had been suffering from a big deficit before the start of the second half, but they had put together a little mini-run to cut it down to size. Yet when Durant tried to send a message to the Lakers and their fans by finishing the break-away play in stunning fashion, their veteran opponents had a statement of their own to make.

"Bad pass through the hands of Gasol.... Durant... BLOCKED BY BRYANT!" the Laker announcer exclaimed in joy, echoing the excitement by the Laker home fans. Just when the Thunder thought they could pull closer, Kobe Bryant ruthlessly halted them in their tracks, swatting away Kevin Durant's layup attempt with an emphatic thud.

There was simply no stopping the veteran, experienced and battle-tested Lakers' onslaught against the young and naïve Thunder team. Being the defending champions, and having had decades' worth of basketball experience on one team, the Lakers were everything the Thunder were not - but they were everything the Thunder aspired to be: experienced, ruthless, edgy, and most importantly champions. It was a gut-wrenching, heartbreaking series for the Thunder, eventually losing in six games, while the Lakers eventually won the NBA Championship that year once again.

Kevin was finally aware of an entirely new, invisible game being played around him – a higher level of basketball required to reach immortality and greatness. He was as hungry as ever to reach that level. He was ready to grow from just being the talented college kid who could score the ball with an effortless ease. He was ready to face the realm of NBA legends head on, and conquer his rightful place on the throne by any means necessary. Yet as K.D. had always experienced throughout his life, whenever he aspired to reach any goal he would face immense setbacks. Being the underdog throughout his entire life, he would have to battle against all odds to achieve his goals.

The battle to the top of basketball's biggest stage would be the hardest and the most grueling challenge number 35 would have to endure in his NBA career – but it was nothing that Kevin Durant wasn't ready for.

CHAPTER TEN

GROWING PAINS

"With everything I do, I just try to be myself." – Kevin Durant

THE FIRST TASTE OF THE PLAYOFFS for the young Thunder team had them hooked, and after having experienced their first high from that whole other level of the game, they were now addicted – willing to do everything in their power to get back to the playoffs. A season had passed since their untimely demise against the Lakers, but they were now hungrier than ever to take the spoils of success for themselves. K.D. had spent the offseason working on his game tirelessly, improving every facet of his skills as much as he could. His teammates had also gotten better, and with a more developed team around him, the Thunder managed to win an impressive 55 games the following year, with Durant once again taking home the scoring title.

https://www.flickr.com/photos/keithallison/12274944504/

What was once their weakness had turned into a strength. They had always been "too young" or "too inexperienced" to win on the NBA's biggest stage, but with all the elite teams not getting any younger and with the

Thunder having garnered a couple of good years of experience under their belt, they suddenly seemed in a more prime position to win than they had ever been before. Their youth would serve them as an advantage over the veteran teams, out jumping, out-hustling and just being overall more athletic than their opponents. With this new arsenal of weapons available to them, Kevin would make a series of impressively deep playoff runs with his young team.

The NBA landscape was experiencing a power shift of epic proportions – one that had not been seen in years. The defending champions, the Lakers, were declining and suddenly all hope for a three-peat had dissipated. The Miami Heat had just acquired a superstar in LeBron James, and they had now become heavily favored to win an NBA title, whilst other veteran teams such as the Dallas Mavericks and Boston Celtics still had a few years of good playing time left to them but were slowly declining as well. Once again it seemed like everyone had forgotten about Kevin and the Thunder. They were good, and they were improving, but they were not the headline grabbers that all the other elite teams were. Things were quiet in OKC, but Kevin was used to quiet by now – and just like how he had always done throughout his career, he would let his game do most of the talking.

2011 Western Conference Finals Game 1. One year fresh from their playoff debacle to the Lakers, the Thunder came back strong and found themselves in the Western Conference Finals against the aging Dallas Mavericks, led by their superstar Dirk Nowitzki. The Mavs had surprised everyone, dismantling the defending champion Lakers in astounding fashion and sweeping them in their four game series; they were now vying for the Western Conference Title. The Mavs and Thunder were polar opposites, with the

Mavericks being the experienced, aging veterans with the Thunder the young, athletic group. However different they may be, they were both similar in one aspect – they were hungry, championship-deprived teams, desperate for one shot to win the coveted NBA Championship. Once again, K.D. found himself up against an experienced and battle-tested team just like he had been against the Lakers. The spotlight was now all on him, and everyone was speculating as to whether he had truly grown and matured enough to defeat such a team – a feat they had failed to do so the year before.

Durant was confident in his ability, and having shattered doubts by rising above all expectations and leading his team to the brink of the NBA Finals, the Thunder were on a roll and experiencing the peak of the high that they were still so addicted to. The Mavs on the other hand had struggled year-in and year-out to make it past the 2nd round or the

Conference Finals, always falling short of their ultimate goal. And with aging, veteran players on their roster, it would only be a matter of time before they were out of playoff contention for good. It was a now-or-never situation for the Mavs, and they had everything to lose – players, legacies, hopes and dreams; meanwhile the Thunder had everything to gain. The Mavericks had their backs up against the wall, while the Thunder were rising through the ranks with seemingly effortless dominance. Kevin had finally thought that that year would be the year where he would shed his underdog persona for good, but unfortunately for him, history was doomed to repeat itself once more. Despite everything going in the Thunder's favor, they would find themselves coming up short against a veteran, experienced, and battle-tested team once again – perfectly punctuated by a historical performance from their leader, Dirk Nowitzki.

CHAPTER ELEVEN

A FAMILIAR LOSS

"I've learned what it feels like to lose, believe me. But I think, in the end, that is just going to make winning that much better." – Kevin Durant

SECONDS TICKED OFF THE CLOCK after the opening tip. Without any hesitation, the ball made its way into Dirk's hands. Guarding him was Serge Ibaka, a player known for his defensive prowess and blocking ability. But Ibaka certainly wasn't prepared for the offensive massacre that he was about to undergo throughout the course of the next 48 minutes. Dirk sized him up and casually rose into one of his patented, signature one-legged fadeaway jump shots.

"And there's that tremendous shooter in Dirk Nowitzki again," the commentator pre-empting the offensive brilliance that was about to ensue after Dirk hit down his first jump shot with ease. Seconds later, Dirk had the ball in his hands once more, and was once again sizing up Ibaka.

"Here's Ibaka on Nowitzki...Spins AROUND HIM AND THROWS IT DOWN!" Dirk pulled off a spectacular baseline spin move and threw down a fanciful dunk right on the Thunder's defense, leaving Ibaka in the dust. The Mavs were already on the board with 6 points, and all of them had come from the Mavs' German leader – foreshadowing the outcome of the game as well as the night Nowitzki was about to have.

"Nowitzki.... AGAIN! 3 for 3, 8 points already!" The commentator announced to the world, which by that point already knew that Dirk was heating up and that he was in for a special type of night. Kevin Durant had sensed that the game was not going his way, and while being in an opponent's arena, with their leading superstar about to single-handedly dismantle them, he would try his very best to reel his team back into contention.

K.D. decided to pull a page out of Dirk's playbook and began hitting a couple of fade away jump shots as well on his opponents.

Suddenly, what was supposed to be a walkover victory for the Thunder had turned into a back-and-forth duel between a veteran superstar and a rising phenom. Dirk and K.D. both put on stellar shooting performances and were both leading their teams in scoring. Dirk was hitting almost all of his impossible shots and Durant followed closely behind.

Time was winding down in the first quarter, and the duel between Dirk and Kevin was going full swing – with fans from all over the world loving the showdown they were witnessing. Here were two superstars, both at different times of their career, but both battling and vying extremely hard for the same coveted trophy.

JJ Barea, a Mavs guard, sliced his way into the lane for a floater to end the 1st quarter, only for the ball to hit the back off the rim and fall into the hands of Durant. With only 6 seconds left to spare, K.D. blazed across the floor, all the way to the other side of the court to lay in a buzzer-beating basket - ending the first quarter off in style and giving the Thunder the lead. The momentum, for a split second, seemed to shift towards the Thunder's side, and the collective relief on the Thunder team was apparent as they high fived one another for their first quarter effort. For a brief moment it seemed that the Thunder might have been able to actually win the game, showing complete disregard for whatever team they were facing no matter how experienced they were or whether or not their star player was having an incredible shooting night. Little did they know that their celebration would be short-lived.

Veteran teams have been through so many NBA games and situations that they know a momentary lead does and will not determine the eventual outcome of the game. Dirk, with all his years of experience and greatness, would teach Durant and the Thunder that harsh and brutal lesson the hard way.

Fast forward a couple of moments into the game, and the Mavs fans were screaming ecstatically. The Mavericks were relishing in the moment, high-fiving one another after having gone through an intense run of battling back. "Nowitzki.... Cutting to the basket.... AND A FOUL!" Dirk had not stopped his reign of terror on the Thunder; not having missed a single field goal, and just scoring an aggressive layup while earning the foul, gave him the potential 3-point play and more importantly the lead over the Thunder. By now, Durant knew the Mavs weren't messing around; if the Thunder were to defeat them, it would require much more than just a simple momentum shift. The Mavericks had been title contenders for years, and now K.D. knew exactly what made them so. Kevin once again tried to buckle down and lead his team over the hump, but by then it was too late. The momentum had shifted too far away, Dirk was absolutely unstoppable, and the

Mavs fans were booing the Thunder players out of their arena.

4th quarter, and whatever efforts by Durant to will his team back had been drowned out by Dirk's astounding playoff performance. Now up by 7 with about a minute left to play, Dirk would once again stab the dagger in the Thunder's hearts, hammering the final nail in the coffin and putting an end to his spectacular Game 1 performance.

"Nowitzki...IT'S GOOD! WOAH! 46 POINTS!!" Dirk once again nailed a fade away jumper over Serge Ibaka, and by then, everyone knew the game was a done deal. The announcer could not hold back his excitement any longer after watching the brilliant show put on by Dirk Nowitzki, and the fans shared the same excitement, cheering for their team in jubilation. The only ones who weren't in on the celebrations were K.D. and his team. With their heads down, they headed to the locker room, spirits crushed and dreams broken. What was supposed to be Kevin's opportunity to make a definitive mark on the league was once again denied to him; for the rest of the series, Kevin Durant and the Thunder would lose their share of the spotlight to the Dallas Mavericks.

CHAPTER TWELVE

NICE GUYS DON'T FINISH LAST

"I'm busy working on every aspect of my game – defense, shooting, rebounding – but I really want to become a better overall team player. Help my teammates become better players out on the court in order to win more ball games." – Kevin Durant

DIRK NOWITZKI, THE GERMAN SUPERSTAR AND LEADER of the Mavericks, would replace Kobe's role in halting the Thunder in their tracks – showing them exactly why they were not ready to win a championship. The world had witnessed a historic performance by the Dirk, but they had also witnessed yet another Thunder embarrassment. It was a spectacle for the ages – one from the awe-inspiring performance by the German, and one from the disappointing debacle by the Oklahoma City Thunder.

The Mavs would eventually win the series against the Thunder in 5 games, and also pull off one of the greatest upsets in NBA Finals history by defeating the superstar-loaded Miami Heat. Once again, Durant. would have to sit out the remaining time of his offseason as the league's underdog – only being able to stare up at the glorious NBA summit while another team reigned victorious from it.

Broken, tired and deflated, Kevin had simply had enough. He went into seclusion for a couple of days. He needed to get his mind right and get his game back on track. He had always been the NBA's Nice Guy, and he had built his reputation and legacy around that very image. But that legacy seemed to be working against him. Many analysts wondered if Kevin had the cold-blooded tenacity required of a player to win a championship or whether he would forever be destined to playoff disappointment. Setbacks weren't something foreign to K.D., having had to fight against all odds to get to where he was at that moment. He had succeeded before against all doubts and haters, and this time, he would be determined to do so again.

Undeterred, he was determined to prove that nice guys don't always finish last.

CHAPTER THIRTEEN

SECOND BEST

"I've been second my whole life. I was the second best player in high school. I was the second pick in the draft. I've been second in MVP voting three times. I came second in the Finals. I'm tired of being second. I'm done with it." – Kevin Durant

KEVIN WAS SITTING OPPOSITE THE REPORTER for yet another interview – one of many that he had experienced throughout his career by that point. Showtime Sports was running the interview, and they decided to have a 60-minute special on the superstar. The reporter began by reciting Durant's highly talked about statement that he was tired of being second best.

After reciting almost verbatim the exact words that K.D. had said about his unfortunate yet consistent placing in today's NBA, he was then asked if he still stood by those words.

Kevin paused, and with a stone cold demeanor replied to the reporter: "Definitely."

His emotion was clear in his response. He had nearly rolled his eyes in exhaustion when answering the question, almost as if he was letting out all those years of pent up frustration rage. Being second had begun to wear on Durant – he had had to live with that label for the majority of his life. He'd always been the underdog, always been overlooked and always been underappreciated, but he had never complained about his circumstances, and in fact he would not have developed the work ethic and discipline that led him to where he was today without experiencing such struggle. Yet despite his rise to prominence in the NBA, he was still seemingly unable to shake off the shackles of his past – and although having played close to a decade now in the NBA, he was still facing his demons of being merely "second."

In high school, Greg Oden beat him out for the number one spot. In the NBA draft, he was once again selected second after Oden. In the NBA, he would always finish 2nd in MVP voting behind LeBron James, currently deemed the best player in the world. Most recently, and perhaps most painfully, he would finish second in the NBA Finals, once again behind LeBron James, and once again having the opportunity to win his ultimate prize be denied to him so mercilessly.

NBA Finals

The 2012 NBA Finals had the Thunder

matched up against the heavily scrutinized Miami Heat. The Oklahoma City Thunder, after what seemed like a constant battle for relevance in the Western Conference for close to 5 years, had amazingly pulled off a historical playoff run. All those previous years they had been denied in the playoffs, whether to the Lakers, the Mavericks or other veteran teams, certainly had had a positive effect on the team; as the following year, they managed to pull through with gutsy series wins over both the Mavs and the Lakers, as well as the veteran San Antonio Spurs. The Thunder had finally seemed to have learned from their past inexperience matching up against those teams, conquering them in spectacular fashion. They advanced to the highest level of the NBA playoffs.

It was truly a run for the ages. A young team, led by their young superstar, having been denied of all their chances to win basketball's biggest prize, finally earned their shot at winning a championship. Kevin was naturally over the moon,when he hoisted the Western Conference Finals trophy over head to the clamor of his adoring OKC Thunder fans. The city of Oklahoma had always been infamous for its natural disasters and the general negative media consensus surrounding it, but for once Kevin had given the people in Oklahoma something new and bright to hope for – sporting glory and immortality.

For a young, small-market team, the Thunder certainly did not lack any maturity, teamwork or skill in their short stint of development as a franchise. They had always been a quiet, subtle team compared to all the other big-market teams out there in the league, and there was no better representative of their franchise than the humblest and perhaps quietest superstar in the NBA. Kevin had always let his game do most of the talking, and reaching the NBA Finals was the pinnacle of that very success. One more hurdle remained for K.D. to be deemed truly victorious, his ultimate goal of winning a championship – the NBA Finals. Many reporters felt the Thunder playoff run that year to be similar to that of a fairy tale for how they managed to defy all expectations and lay siege to their opponents in a beautiful heroic tale. However, that fairy tale would not have a happy ending.

2012 NBA Finals, Game 1.

"Here comes Durant... to the basket... LAUNCHES AND FIRES IT DOWN!" The announcer screamed, partly from excitement, but also partly to have his voice heard over the roaring Thunder fans drowning out all the other noise in the arena.

Kevin had gotten hold of the loose ball after a timely interception by his teammates, sprinted down with lightning quick speed, and dunked the ball to the delight of the fans. Everybody in the Thunder home arena was on their feet, high-fiving and cheering their squad, celebrating the effort K.D. had put on to battle from 13 down to take a 5 point lead in exciting fashion. The momentum had completely swung 180 degrees, and it was all Kevin and the Thunder, surging and putting the Heat's backs against the wall. Flashes of brilliance were seen in Durant akin to his college game against OSU where he single-handedly led his team back into contention.

"Durant for three…. BANG!" K.D. once again responded to the Miami Heat's defense by launching a deadly 3-pointer, extending their lead, driving it closer and closer to double digits.

They just had to keep their surge going for a couple of more minutes. It would only be a matter of time before the Thunder could claim victory.

When his team needed a dagger to seal the game for good, Kevin would answer the call and step up to the plate once again. "Durant again.... Knocks it down! 13 points in the 4th!" K.D. had extended the Thunder's lead to 8 points, and with all the momentum on their side plus only a couple of minutes left to the game, the Thunder had successfully sealed a beautiful Game 1 victory in the NBA Finals.

Kevin held his head high in pride, for it seemed for that brief moment, the Thunder's fairy tale playoff run continued. His hopes for a championship were shining brighter than ever, and for once he thought his unlucky streak with being second best was about to come to an end. Reminding the world of the brilliance he possessed as a player, that Game 1 victory was a statement to the world that Kevin Durant was just as great of a baller as anyone, and that he deserved to win the championship just as much as any other player out there. However, one game wouldn't be enough to solidify Kevin's hopes and dreams. He had taken the first step in

moving past the final hurdle towards h[...]
but he needed to win three more games
claim the victory he so desparately wanted.

Yet history proved to be a cruel foe to
Kevin time and time again. Unfortunately, he
would find himself just short of his coveted
trophy once more.

Game 5. With time ticking away, and
seconds left in the game, all of LeBron James'
fans had waited years to be able to utter the
word "champion" beside his name. After close
to a decade in LeBron's career, the announcer
finally took the words out of their mouths,
ending their suspense for good: "The Miami
Heat, are once again NBA Champions,
LeBron James captures that elusive title he so
desperately coveted."

This would be the leading news headline
all across the world. Once again, Kevin found
himself overshadowed, forgotten by the glory
of another player's success. He had come so

3A journey, and with his ultimate

n view of his reach, it was cruelly

im once again by another better

re   formidable   opponent.

Heartbreakingly for Durant, he was still the underdog of the league – still number two.

A couple of moments before the buzzer sounded and LeBron was seen hugging K.D. at the scorer's table. Confetti began to fly down on them, celebrating LeBron's victory and seemingly mocking and patronizing Durant's failure at the same time. It was a moment LeBron had been waiting for his entire career, the one thing the public had been critical of him up to that point was not being able to win an NBA Title. Finally, LeBron could put those demons to rest, whereas Kevin would still be stuck battling his own.

The Heat would go on to win 4 games in a row against the Thunder after their Game 1 defeat, putting an anti-climactic end to the

Thunder's inspiring story to the top. Even though everything had gone so well for him throughout his entire playoff run, K.D. still begrudgingly found himself in second place. LeBron had outdueled and outperformed Kevin in many aspects, and in the end, he was the evident victor. Durant could only walk to the locker room, a towel over his head, looking down in disappointment, and hug his mother who was waiting to support him - just as she had done for all his life. Losing in the Finals was the pinnacle of heartbreak and just yet another instance of suffering that painful trend in his career.

However, if there was one thing apparent in K.D.'s life that all of his past defeats had in common, it was that he never settled for the place or circumstance he was put in. The world may have him at number two, but he would always defy their expectations, showcasing his heart of a champion – regardless of whether the world thought he was one or not. He had proven not just to the world but also to himself that number two was merely a limit that he did not have to live by – always rising above the second place expectation that people seemed to constantly put on him.

Despite being the second best player out of high school, he still made basketball relevant for a college that was known predominantly for its football program. Despite being drafted second, he would still go on to win the Rookie of the Year Award. And despite him coming up second in the Finals, nobody doubted Kevin Durant's ability to bounce back, grow and develop for another shot at basketball immortality. Finally, despite coming up second place in MVP voting three times, he finally broke through past his second place position in 2014, winning the MVP trophy as well as hearts all around the world.

CHAPTER FOURTEEN

#1 SPOT

"My time is now." – Kevin Durant

2014 NBA MVP AWARD ACCEPTANCE CEREMONY. Back to the podium where Kevin was still giving his emotional MVP acceptance speech. Anyone listening was given a glimpse into Durant's life up to that point, as he led them down memory lane - sharing the moments that had made him the man and MVP that he had grown into over the years. His early life struggles, to his rise to stardom; his summit of the NBA to the building of his Nice Guy reputation; his legacy in the league thus far; his status, once forever heralded as being the second best, would no longer be an apt description. He was now deemed the Most Valuable Player in the league, and nothing less.

His cathartic speech gave way to a flood of emotions that filled the room – so many highs and lows in one single moment, all indicative of the ones Kevin had faced throughout his storied career and life. As he wrapped up his final thank yous towards his friends and family, one could not help but wonder what else Kevin Durant had in store for his fans with so many years left in the tank. With eyes still teary from his speech, and an MVP trophy now firmly in his hands, he looked over at the audience in attendance, his team beside him, his family below him and at the fans watching from all over the world – still the same poverty-stricken, humble kid from Washington, DC. He was still the same underdog that everybody doubted when rising through the league, still the same superstar that everybody had grown to love and respect, and still the same Kevin Durant that will be vying, bleeding and dying for that #1 spot in basketball glory for the years to come.

He had been recognized as the best and the most valuable player in the world. All he had left was one more goal, one more #1 spot to claim – the one that he had failed to do so two years prior to his award acceptance, but the one that he certainly would not be undeterred by any longer. He had now garnered all the motivation and support in the world to pursue his goals with even more vigor; after showing his vulnerability to the NBA audience, he could not have possibly be showered with anymore love and admiration than he had already received after his moving speech.

With tears still in his eyes, he set his sights on that ever-elusive prize. He walked off the stage quietly, more determined than ever to proceed back to work.

https://www.flickr.com/photos/keithallison/12272160823/

Thanks for reading! Please add a short review on Amazon, and let me know what you thought!

You can also find my other books about other basketball legends on Amazon.

John Emerson

Made in the USA
San Bernardino, CA
17 November 2017